THE PRINCESS AND THE PEA, NO TV, AND OTHER PLAYS

Four Short Plays for Children
by
RIC AVERILL

Columbia College Library
600 South Michigan
Chicago, IL 60605

Dramatic Publishing
Woodstock, Illinois • London, England • Melbourne, Australia

812.54 A952p

Averill, Ric.

The princess and the pea, No TV, and other plays

*** NOTICE ***

The amateur and stock acting rights to this work are controlled exclusively by THE DRAMATIC PUBLISHING COMPANY without whose permission in writing no performance of it may be given. Royalty fees are given in our current catalog and are subject to change without notice. Royalty must be paid every time a play is performed whether or not it is presented for profit and whether or not admission is charged. A play is performed any time it is acted before an audience. All inquiries concerning amateur and stock rights should be addressed to:

DRAMATIC PUBLISHING
P. O. Box 129, Woodstock, Illinois 60098

COPYRIGHT LAW GIVES THE AUTHOR OR THE AUTHOR'S AGENT *THE EXCLUSIVE RIGHT TO MAKE COPIES.* This law provides authors with a fair return for their creative efforts. Authors earn their living from the royalties they receive from book sales and from the performance of their work. Conscientious observance of copyright law is not only ethical, it encourages authors to continue their creative work. This work is fully protected by copyright. No alterations, deletions or substitutions may be made in the work without the prior written consent of the publisher. No part of this work may be reproduced or transmitted in any form or by any means, electronic or mechanical, including photocopy, recording, videotape, film, or any information storage and retrieval system, without permission in writing from the publisher. It may not be performed either by professionals or amateurs without payment of royalty. All rights, including but not limited to the professional, motion picture, radio, television, videotape, foreign language, tabloid, recitation, lecturing, publication, and reading are reserved.

For performance of any songs and recordings mentioned in this play which are in copyright, the permission of the copyright owners must be obtained or other songs and recordings in the public domain substituted.

©MCMXCIX by
RIC AVERILL

Printed in the United States of America
All Rights Reserved
(THE PRINCESS AND THE PEA, NO TV, AND OTHER PLAYS)

ISBN 0-87129-926-7

IMPORTANT BILLING AND CREDIT REQUIREMENTS

All producers of the play *must* give credit to the author(s) of the play in all programs distributed in connection with performances of the play and in all instances in which the title of the play appears for purposes of advertising, publicizing or otherwise exploiting the play and/or a production. The name of the author(s) *must* also appear on a separate line, on which no other name appears, immediately following the title, and *must* appear in size of type not less than fifty percent the size of the title type. Biographical information on the author(s), if included in this book, may be used on all programs. *On all programs this notice must appear:*

"Produced by special arrangement with
THE DRAMATIC PUBLISHING COMPANY of Woodstock, Illinois"

For Trish, my Princess
For Will, the Great One
and, of course,
For Jeanne, my Muse

THE PRINCESS AND THE PEA, NO TV, AND OTHER PLAYS

Contents

The Princess and the Pea 6
No TV 30
Cats and Bats 48
The Great Alphabet Robbery 59

THE PRINCESS AND THE PEA was first produced by the Seem-To-Be-Players for a Kansas tour in the fall of 1998 with the following cast and crew:

Director	JENNIFER GLENN
Music composed and performed by	RIC AVERILL
Costumes	RIC AVERILL
Sets	MARK REANEY, BRENT OLIVER

Prince	CAM DEVICTOR
Queen	JENNIFER GLENN
Page	JERRY MITCHELL
Wizard	JASON WARE
Princess Rose	ERIN KESSLER
Princesses Nettle/ Ivy/ Briar	KIRSTEN PALUDAN

THE PRINCESS AND THE PEA

CHARACTERS

PRINCE
QUEEN: His mother.
PAGE: Their messenger (male or female).
WIZARD
PRINCESS ROSE: A beautiful young maiden.
PRINCESS NETTLE: A greedy young maiden.
PRINCESS IVY: A needy young maiden.
PRINCESS BRIAR: A bossy young maiden.

>PLACE: In a kingdom faraway.
>TIME: Long ago.

SETTING: *Lights come up on a unit set. Castle spires in the background inform the audience that the chambers before them are royal, complete with a throne and a grand entrance slightly UL. DL is an archway that leads to a bedchamber. UR are steps leading up to an overlook near one of the castle spires. DR is an archway that leads to a small area which serves as "outdoors," with a tree overhanging a small clearing. The action moves from the castle chamber to outside and back again, with the next to last short scene in the royal bedroom.*

AT RISE: *PRINCE enters. He is very young and handsome, but sad. He looks around and sighs.*

PRINCE. Ahhh. Empty. The room is empty. The castle is empty. My life is empty. *(Sighs again.)* Ahhh.

(PRINCE turns, walks up the steps to the overlook and leans on his elbows, looking very winsome. PAGE enters. PAGE is enthusiastic and somewhat cocky.)

PAGE. Prince! Prince? Where are you? *(PAGE looks about, pokes his head into the bedchamber. Runs back into the room and looks out the front door, shakes his head.)*
PRINCE *(sighs)*. Ahhh. *(PAGE hears him, runs to the bottom of the steps.)*
PAGE. Ha, there you are. Fishing today, Your Majesty?
PRINCE *(sighs)*. Ahhh.
PAGE *(shrugs)*. Chess, perhaps?
PRINCE *(sighs)*. Ahhh.
PAGE *(runs to bedroom, looks in)*. A nap?
PRINCE *(looking down, finally noticing PAGE)*. Is that my Page making so much noise?
PAGE. Indeed, Your Majesty. Your first Page, your last Page, your one and only Page. I'm the whole book.
PRINCE. I really don't want company and I don't want to play. I just...I just want to look over the ramparts and... *(Sighs.)* Ahhh.
PAGE *(shakes his head)*. Something is wrong with you. Something is definitely wrong with you. I'm going to go get the Court Wizard. He'll know what to do. *(He runs out the UL entrance.)*
PRINCE. I don't want anybody to *do* anything. I just want to be left alone. *(Sighs.)* Ahhh.

(PAGE enters UL with the Court WIZARD. PAGE is talking.)

PAGE. ...doesn't want company, doesn't want to play. He just wants to look over the ramparts and... Ahhh. *(Sighs, imitating the PRINCE, who sighs immediately after.)*

PRINCE. Ahhh.

PAGE. You see?

WIZARD. Ah, I do, I do see. I always see. That's my job, you know, I'm a seer. And being a seer, I'm also a believer. And I believe I know the root of this boy's problem. Yes, the root is known and we can pluck it out, or cure it at least. Page, go and get the Queen. I'll stay here with the boy. *(PAGE exits.)*

PRINCE *(looks down at WIZARD, who returns his gaze)*. I don't need anyone to stay with me, Wizard. I don't need any of your spells.

WIZARD. Ha, you may think not, but I know the root of your problem and it will make you wildly unpredictable, mark my words, and I do mark my own words, which is why I have so many books in my chambers.

(QUEEN enters UL, ushered in by the PAGE.)

QUEEN. What is it, what is it? It must be important to bring me away from tea before crumpets. *(She notices her son.)* Why are you up there, my Prince?

WIZARD & PAGE. He doesn't want company, he doesn't want to play, he just wants to look over the ramparts and— *(They sigh.)* Ahhh.

QUEEN *(stops them)*. Cut that out! What is going on, son?

PRINCE. They're right, Mother. I just want to be left alone.

QUEEN. Left alone? Left alone? By all of us?

PRINCE. I believe that's what alone is.

WIZARD. Queen, I think I know the problem, and knowing that, I think I know the solution, and knowing that, I think the problem's solved.

PAGE. Not yet, Wizard, the boy's still up there.

QUEEN. Yes, yes, Wizard, what do you think is the problem?

WIZARD. Adolescence, my dear Queen. The boy has a severe and crisis case of adolescence.

QUEEN. My goodness. Already?

WIZARD. I'm afraid so.

PAGE. Is it catching?

WIZARD. It's inevitable.

PAGE. I'm not going up there.

QUEEN. But what can be done?

WIZARD. It's really quite simple. For now, we must leave him alone. But the ultimate solution is to get him a bride.

PAGE. A bride? Scary.

QUEEN. A princess around the castle? Is it really time, Wizard?

WIZARD. I'm afraid so, Your Majesty.

QUEEN. Then so be it. Page!

PAGE. Yes, Your Majesty?

QUEEN. Go out across the kingdom and proclaim that as soon as we find the perfect princess, the Prince shall take her for his bride and they shall one day be the rulers of this fair kingdom.

PAGE. Yes, Your Majesty.

QUEEN. Come, Wizard, let us continue to experiment with your elixir of youth. I suddenly feel very old. *(She and WIZARD exit. PAGE looks up at PRINCE.)*

PAGE. Uh, Prince, any special requests in princess types?

PRINCE *(looks down at him)*. Just leave me alone, please. I don't care about anything. I just want to be left alone. *(Sighs.)* Ahhh.

(PAGE shrugs and starts out the DR archway. The lights shift and music moves us forward in time. PRINCESS ROSE enters with milk pails. PAGE stops near her.)

PAGE. Hear ye! Hear ye! The Prince will take a bride. All perfect princesses should apply. Hear ye! Hear ye! *(He stops and looks at ROSE.)* Hello, ye. What are you doing?

PRINCESS ROSE. Silly Page. I've just milked a cow for a poor old woman whose joints were too knobby to do it herself.

PAGE. Yuck. My joints are knobby, too. May I have a sip? *(ROSE smiles and offers him a bucket. He drinks.)* Do you know where any perfect princesses are?

PRINCESS ROSE. I don't know that any princess is perfect. Princess Nettle lives just over that hill, and I—

PAGE. Over the hill. My thanks, milkmaid. Uh, back to work. *(He exits, ROSE smiles and looks up at the castle.)*

PRINCESS ROSE. If I lived in that castle, someone else would do the milking for me. *(Sighs.)* Ahhh.

(ROSE leaves just as PAGE enters with PRINCESS NETTLE. He is moving in front of her as if in retreat.)

PRINCESS NETTLE. Tell me more, Page. How big is the royal tiara? Are the bedrooms nice? Satin sheets? How big is this kingdom anyway? And—

PAGE. Please, please, I'm only a Page. Not even a very interesting or important Page, so save your questions for the Queen and the Prince. *(They enter the DL archway and PAGE cries out.)* Hear ye! Hear ye! Princess Nettle is here to meet the Prince.

(QUEEN enters with the WIZARD behind her.)

PRINCE *(looks down and sighs).* Ahhh. *(Looks away.)*

PRINCESS NETTLE *(curtsies deeply).* Your Majesty. I'm a perfect princess here to apply to be your loyal daughter-in-law.

QUEEN. Oh, my, what manners. *(QUEEN curtsies back. WIZARD and PAGE bow. NETTLE curtsies again. QUEEN responds in kind. NETTLE curtsies yet again, even lower. QUEEN tries to imitate, gets stuck, WIZARD and PAGE pull her back up.)* I am charmed, Princess Nettle. Tell me, what are your ambitions as princess? What do you desire?

PRINCESS NETTLE. Why, everything, Your Majesty, of course. I want treasure and baubles and dresses and land and more land and more treasures and dances and everything fine. *(QUEEN nods to WIZARD who nods to the PAGE who is shaking his head no, but upon seeing the nods, he nods his head.)*

QUEEN. Done! Just go up those steps and introduce yourself to the Prince and as soon as he agrees, we'll have the wedding and he will sigh no more.

The Princess and the Pea 13

PRINCESS NETTLE. Thank you, Your Majesty. *(She walks up the steps. PRINCE looks at her as she reaches his platform.)*

PRINCE *(sighs).* Ahhh. Hello. Who are you?

PRINCESS NETTLE. I'm Nettle, your perfect princess. Just think, it won't be long before your mother is gone and then you'll be king and I'll be your perfect queen and we shall have everything and what we don't have we will take or tax the people so we can buy it and then we'll have everything, everything, everything—

PRINCE. But love?

PRINCESS NETTLE. Love?

PRINCE. I'm sorry, Princess Nettle, but I really just want to be left alone. *(Sighs and turns away.)* Ahhh. *(NETTLE walks back down and looks dumbstruck at QUEEN and WIZARD.)*

QUEEN. What did he say? When is the wedding to be?

PRINCESS NETTLE. He wants...he wants to be left alone.

QUEEN. What does that mean?

WIZARD *(whispering in QUEEN's ear).* It means he doesn't love her, and not loving her, he doesn't want her.

PAGE *(also whispering).* It means she's not the perfect princess after all.

PRINCESS NETTLE *(looks at all of them, indignantly realizing what's happening).* How dare you, any of you! I'm too good for this tiny kingdom anyway. I'm going to go find a more perfect prince somewhere else. Good day! *(She stomps off.)*

QUEEN. Oh, my, she wasn't perfect at all. Now what?

WIZARD. We keep searching, and searching we find, and finding we—

QUEEN. Page!
PAGE. I'm on my way!

(QUEEN and WIZARD exit. PAGE goes DR through the archway as lights shift. ROSE enters carrying a tray of baked goods. PAGE stops near her.)

PAGE. Hear ye! Hear ye! Hello, ye! I remember you. The Prince will take a bride and all perfect princesses should apply. What goodies do you have there?
PRINCESS ROSE. Silly Page. Just sweetmeats and bread pudding. I made them for a poor princess who's feeling ill.
PAGE. Uh, I'm feeling ill?
PRINCESS ROSE. Here, you can have one. But just one.
PAGE *(devours a cake)*. Made these for a princess? Where is she? And is she perfect?
PRINCESS ROSE. I don't know that any princess is perfect. But her name is Princess Ivy and she lives just down the vale. I might mention that I am also—
PAGE. Down the vale. Here, I'll take these for you! *(PAGE exits, eating another cake.)*
PRINCESS ROSE *(smiles and sighs, looks up at the castle)*. Ahhh. If I lived there, they'd have a huge kitchen and I might not have to do all the cooking, but what I did cook, I'd cook for someone special. *(Sighs.)* Ahhh.

(ROSE turns and exits. PAGE enters with PRINCESS IVY. He is walking beside her listening to her whine and complain.)

PRINCESS IVY. There were supposed to be more cakes on the tray. She always brings more cakes. How come there aren't more cakes?

PAGE. Please, please, I'm only a simple Page. When you get to the castle there will be more cakes than you can imagine. *(They enter the DR archway and PAGE cries out.)* Hear ye! Hear ye! Princess Ivy is here to meet the Prince.

(QUEEN enters with the WIZARD behind her.)

PRINCE *(looks down and sighs, looks back away)*. Ahhh.

PRINCESS IVY *(walks up to the QUEEN)*. Oh, you must be the Queen. You're so pretty. I wish I could be just like you. I never had a mother that I can remember and I've been ever so, ever so lonely. *(Throws her arms around the QUEEN, almost in tears.)*

QUEEN. Oh, my, what an affectionate child. *(QUEEN nods to WIZARD and PAGE, who peels her off.)* Do you think you could be a perfect princess for my son the Prince?

PRINCESS IVY. Just tell me what to do. I'll be whatever you want, just as long as you feed me and clothe me and keep me from harm. Please, I've been alone so long I was beginning to think no one cared about me. *(She starts to cry and QUEEN comforts her, giving her a hug, which she returns quite strongly.)*

QUEEN. There, there, we care. *(Peeling her off again.)* Now, you just go on up those stairs and talk to the Prince and just as soon as he names the day, then you shall be my daughter. *(QUEEN nods to WIZARD who has been shaking his head no with the PAGE. Upon seeing the QUEEN, they both nod their heads.)*

PRINCESS IVY. I hope he'll like me. What if he doesn't like me?

PAGE. He isn't going to know if he likes you if you don't go up those steps.

WIZARD *(whispering).* I don't hold out much hope for this one, Page. *(QUEEN shoots them a look. IVY walks up the steps. PRINCE looks at her as she reaches his platform.)*

PRINCE *(sighs).* Ahhh. Who are you?

PRINCESS IVY. Oh, don't even say it. I knew it. I knew you wouldn't like me! No one likes me. I can't help it if I whine all the time. It's just that nothing ever goes right and I can't figure out why and then everyone makes fun of me and I want to be perfect, but I know I'm not and I wish I was and now you hate me and I give up... *(She goes back down the stairs, half in tears.)*

PRINCE. She didn't say one word about love. Ahhh. *(Turns away. PRINCESS IVY looks at the QUEEN and the WIZARD, bursts into tears.)*

PRINCESS IVY. He's terrible. He has no sympathy. I don't think anyone will ever marry him. Certainly not I!

QUEEN *(watching her exit in tears through archway DR).* What in the world was that all about?

WIZARD. Your Majesty, I suspect the boy told her that he wants to be left alone, and wanting to be alone means—

QUEEN. He doesn't love her.

PAGE. Still not a perfect princess? *(QUEEN and WIZARD shake their heads and turn to exit.)* I'm on my way!

(PAGE shrugs and starts out the DR archway. The lights shift and music moves us forward in time. ROSE enters and sits, strumming on a lute. She sings. PAGE stops near her to listen. Note: Music is at end of play.)

PRINCESS ROSE.
> Somewhere a-looking, over the sea,
> Somewhere a laddie is looking for me,
> Someday I'll find him, and lovers we'll be,
> This laddie who sighs as he looks o'er the sea.

PAGE. Hello. I hear ye playing so perfectly. That's a fine song. I hate to ask you again, but, I am looking for a perfect princess and you seem to know where the princesses are in this kingdom. Do you think— *(ROSE puts a finger to her lips and he stops talking.)*

PRINCESS ROSE. Silly Page. I've told you twice that there is no such thing as a perfect princess. And I've tried to tell you something else. I am a—

(PRINCESS BRIAR stomps in. She is very bossy and mean. She stares at the PAGE, ignoring ROSE.)

PRINCESS BRIAR. You there! Are you the Page that's been tellin' everyone there's fame and fortune to be had just by being perfect? *(She picks him up by the scruff of the neck.)*

PAGE. Uh, it's a princesses-only kind of proposal.

PRINCESS BRIAR. Princesses only. What do I look like to you? A milkmaid? A baker? A butcher? *(She growls and PAGE starts kicking his legs and squirming.)*

PAGE. No, uh, you look, uh, nearly— *(She growls again, stomps on his foot.)* Perfect. That's what you look. You look perfect.

PRINCESS BRIAR. Then take me to my husband right now! And be quick about it. *(She swats PAGE on the bottom and he runs into the castle. BRIAR growls at ROSE, who just smiles, sighs and moves offstage. BRIAR then follows the PAGE into the castle.)* Hear ye! Hear ye! I'm here, ye!

(QUEEN enters with WIZARD behind her. When they see BRIAR, they step back a pace. PRINCE looks down, does a double take and shakes his head.)

PRINCESS BRIAR. Your Majesty. Where's the Prince I'm supposed to marry.

QUEEN. Uh, my dear... uh, my dear...?

PRINCESS BRIAR. Briar. Princess Briar. Where is he?

QUEEN. Well, uh, actually, uh, Wizard, tell her what we were looking for. *(Pushes WIZARD into BRIAR's path.)*

WIZARD *(looks at her, is daunted)*. Uh, Page, didn't you let her know? *(Pushes PAGE in front of him to face BRIAR.)*

PRINCESS BRIAR. Know what? *(Picks up PAGE by the collar.)*

PAGE. Uh, that we're looking for a perfect princess?

PRINCESS BRIAR. Perfect? Who's to say I'm not perfect, huh? Who? Step up, whoever wants to say it! You, Page? *(BRIAR throws him down. PRINCE is listening to all this and comes down, shocked and somewhat interested.)*

PAGE. No, you look, ulp, perfect to me.

PRINCESS BRIAR. Wizard? *(Leans into his face, then steps on his foot. He grimaces in pain.)*

WIZARD. Uh, very, uh, perfect-please-remove-your-foot.

PRINCESS BRIAR *(she does, then goes to QUEEN)*. You seen anybody better, Queen?

QUEEN *(intimidated)*. Uh, no, but, it's really not up to me. It's really up to—

PRINCE. Up to me, Mother? Who is this woman that bullies her way into our castle? *(All start to talk, BRIAR walks up to him.)*

PRINCESS BRIAR. Princess Briar, your bride to be. We're going to rule this country unless anyone dares say we won't.

PRINCE *(looking into her eyes)*. How about this, then, Princess Briar. I say we won't. Because I don't love you. You see, love makes any imperfection seem perfect and that makes the perfect princess. I simply could never love anyone so bossy as you.

PRINCESS BRIAR. Bossy? You think I'm bossy? Why, I've never been so insulted in my life! *(She starts out the door.)* Bossy. I'll show you bossy! The next person says I'm bossy is going to eat their words, that's what they're going to do. I'll show you bossy. I'll bossy my way right out of here!! *(She is gone. PRINCE, PAGE, QUEEN and WIZARD look at one another.)*

PRINCE. Mother, Wizard, Page. I know you mean well, but perhaps there is no perfect princess for me. So please leave me alone. I'll just sigh, and not play and stare over the ramparts until—

(As he is speaking, ROSE enters through the DR archway. She interrupts.)

PRINCESS ROSE. Excuse me, but I was hoping to speak to the Prince. *(PRINCE looks at her, is dumbstruck. He cannot speak at all. He is in love.)*

QUEEN. Who are you, girl?

WIZARD. This is not a good time for an audience with the Prince.

PAGE. He has a severe case of adolescence.

PRINCESS ROSE. But I am a princess, and I was hoping to speak with him... *(She looks at the PRINCE.)* With you.

PRINCE *(stammers, unable to speak in the presence of her beauty)*. Uh, uh, uh... *(He scrambles up the steps to the rampart and looks out, not able to look at her except with furtive glances.)*

QUEEN. Now what's wrong with him?

WIZARD. The adolescence does this too, Your Majesty. Renders them speechless.

PRINCESS ROSE. I heard that you were trying to find a bride for the Prince.

QUEEN. Yes, well, of course, that's true. But we were looking for a princess.

PRINCESS ROSE. I am a princess. I am Princess Rose. *(QUEEN looks at WIZARD who looks at PAGE.)*

PAGE. I don't think so, Your Majesty. This girl is a milkmaid, a baker.

QUEEN. Ah, an impostor.

WIZARD. Shall I imprison her, change her into a toad? *(PRINCE looks down, very interested, moves down a step to listen.)*

PRINCESS ROSE. Please, please allow me to prove myself. I am a princess, though I am far from perfect.

QUEEN. Then what are you doing here? Didn't you hear the Page? Only perfect princesses need apply.

PRINCESS ROSE. But I don't think anyone is perfect!

WIZARD. Your Majesty, I think that would include you! You've been insulted!

QUEEN. Off with her head!

PAGE. I'll go get the executioner. *(He starts off. PRINCE walks down the steps, stronger now.)*

PRINCE. Stop. Wait. Mother, I believe her. I think she is a princess.

QUEEN. Well, you're certainly not marrying her! She's a milkmaid.

WIZARD. A baker! Neighboring kingdoms will talk, my boy.

PRINCE *(approaches ROSE)*. Why did you milk the cow?

PRINCESS ROSE. For a poor old woman whose joints were too knobby to do it herself. *(A pause.)* And to sip some fresh warm milk myself.

PRINCE. And why did you bake?

PRINCESS ROSE. For a princess who was feeling very ill. *(A pause.)* And I do love my sweets.

PRINCE. Then perhaps you are the princess for me.

PRINCESS ROSE. Perhaps.

PRINCE & PRINCESS ROSE *(sigh)*. Ahhh.

QUEEN *(moving in between them)*. How do we know what she says is true?

PAGE. Your Majesty, she did tell me these same stories when I ran into her on the road.

QUEEN. Still, stories are stories. I won't have any but a true princess sleeping in my house! Off with her head!

PRINCE. Please, Mother, isn't there some kind of test you can give her? *(He reaches out and takes ROSE's hand. She smiles at him.)*

PRINCESS ROSE. Yes, please, anything.

QUEEN *(looks to the WIZARD)*. Wizard?

WIZARD. There is one test, Your Majesty. If the girl is a true princess, she should be able to spend a comfortable night on the royal bed; sleeping a long, full and dreamless sleep.

QUEEN. There it is, then. Page, bring on the royal bed. If she spends the night and has a long and full and dreamless sleep then we will know she is a true princess.

PRINCE *(looking into ROSE's eyes).* Then I may marry her?

PRINCESS ROSE *(looks into his eyes, moves closer to him).* And I may marry you.

PRINCE & PRINCESS ROSE. Ahhh. *(WIZARD separates them. PRINCE walks to the UL entrance to the chamber, looks back at her, then exits.)*

WIZARD. Enough, enough. The true test is about to begin! Page! *(WIZARD exits with the QUEEN. PAGE rolls on the royal bed from the royal chamber, DL.)*

PAGE. There you are, Princess. Sleep well and you can boss me around all you want. I'm sorry I didn't know you were a real princess.

PRINCESS ROSE. I'm sorry they don't believe me. But I never lie, Page. Never.

PAGE. Good night, m'lady. Sleep long and full and dreamless. *(She lies down, PAGE walks to the DR archway and makes an announcement.)* Hear ye! Hear ye! If the Princess Rose sleeps a long and full and dreamless sleep, she will be declared a true princess—

(As he makes this announcement, the three castoff PRINCESSES enter DL and listen.)

PAGE. And she will marry the Prince. And they will live happily— *(PRINCESS BRIAR grabs the PAGE and lifts him as PRINCESS IVY and PRINCESS NETTLE flank him.)*

PRINCESS BRIAR. What's all this about Rose?

PRINCESS IVY. I was supposed to marry the Prince.

PRINCESS NETTLE. I wanted him the most and I was the first.

PAGE. Uh, well, the Wizard has spoken and what's been said can't be unsaid.

PRINCESS BRIAR. You're going to unsaid it, or you're going to be sorry! *(The other two agree.)*

PAGE. Uh, what do you want me to do?

PRINCESS BRIAR. Get the Queen out here. We want a better test.

PRINCESS IVY. Yes, prove she's a real princess!

PRINCESS NETTLE. And when she fails, we'll each take a turn.

PRINCESS BRIAR. So speak up! Get the Queen!

PAGE. All right. Queen! Queen! We have visitors!

(QUEEN comes out. She looks at visitors.)

QUEEN. What is going on?

PRINCESS BRIAR. You're being fooled, Your Majesty.

PRINCESS IVY. She's not a true princess and you're not giving her a true test.

QUEEN. No? What's not true about it?

PRINCESS NETTLE. It's too easy. *(Whispers with the other PRINCESSES, making a plan.)* Why not stack up twelve mattresses?

PRINCESS IVY. Yes, twelve soft mattresses.

PRINCESS BRIAR. See if she can sleep on that!

QUEEN. But that would be easier. I don't see—

PRINCESS BRIAR. Not if THIS... *(She reaches into a small bag and pulls out a small green pea.)* ... was underneath the bottom mattress!

QUEEN. A pea? You think she would sleep poorly just because a little dried green pea was at the bottom of a pile of twelve mattresses?

PRINCESS NETTLE. If she's a true princess.

PRINCESS IVY. A true princess would whine and cry and suffer all night.

PRINCESS BRIAR. Are you afraid to try?

QUEEN. Heavens, no. Page.

PAGE. Yes, Your Majesty?

QUEEN. We shall change the royal rules. Stack twelve mattresses on the royal bed and place this pea under the bottom one.

PAGE. Really, Your Majesty?

QUEEN. Yes, really. We shall see if she is a true princess. If she wakes up and claims to have slept well just to get my son, we'll know she is not a true princess.

PRINCESS BRIAR. And if she sleeps fitfully, you can claim she didn't make it one night and then you, Your Majesty, can choose a bride for him.

PRINCESS IVY. Like me.

PRINCESS NETTLE. Or me.

PRINCESS BRIAR. Or the one who had this clever idea. Me?

QUEEN. Page, do my bidding. And you three princesses can spend the night in the guest room. Come along.

(QUEEN leaves with the three PRINCESSES. PAGE goes L and pulls out additional mattresses and walks into ROSE's room. He wakes her.)

The Princess and the Pea 25

PAGE. Princess, Princess. Wake up!

PRINCESS ROSE. Is it morning? I did sleep well. Where is the Prince?

PAGE. Sorry, it's not morning.

PRINCESS ROSE. But—

PAGE. They've changed the royal rules on you. I've got to stack up twelve mattresses and that's all I'm going to say. Here you go. *(He stacks the mattresses and helps her get up on top of them.)* There. Are you comfortable?

PRINCESS ROSE. Yes, I am, I believe. *(As she settles down for the night, he takes the small pea from his pocket and slips it under the bottom mattress.)*

PAGE. Good night, and sweet dreams.

PRINCESS ROSE. Good night, Page. I do hope I sleep well tonight.

(She sighs, lights go down until they are only on the bed. She starts to sleep, then tosses, then turns, aggravated by the tiny pea. The lights go crazy and the music becomes strange. Red lights come up on set as ROSE has a nightmare. In the nightmare, the three other PRINCESSES come out dancing and mock her song from earlier, cackling and laughing.)

PRINCESSES BRIAR, IVY & NETTLE.
    Somewhere a-looking, over the sea,
    Somewhere a prince he is looking for me,
    Someday we'll find him, and lovers we'll be,
    This prince who is looking for me and for me
    and for me and for me.

(Song continues as the PRINCE comes out and they dance around him, then spin him off. They follow. ROSE awakens with a scream. QUEEN comes running in, flanked by BRIAR, IVY and NETTLE. WIZARD, PAGE and PRINCE follow.)

QUEEN. She's awake!
WIZARD. She screams. Did you not sleep well, my child?
PRINCE. Please say you did.
PRINCESS ROSE *(climbing out of the bed)*. There were twelve mattresses, I know, but, but...
PRINCESS NETTLE. Not a true princess.
PRINCESS IVY. Tell the truth.
PRINCESS BRIAR. Did you sleep well?
PRINCESS ROSE. I must tell the truth. I couldn't sleep at all. I'm sorry, my Prince. I slept not at all and I had terrible dreams of witches trying to take you from me.
QUEEN. Just as you would take my son from me. Off you go, milkmaid.
WIZARD. I'm afraid those were the rules.
PRINCE. This can't be true. Page, look at me. Is there some devilment going on here?
PAGE. Uh, sire, the royal rules got changed in the night. The princess was given twelve mattresses to sleep on instead of just one.
PRINCE. No, don't say that!
WIZARD. Sorry, laddie, a true princess should have slept even better on twelve than on one. She's not—
PAGE *(crossing to mattresses, and pulling out the pea)*. *And*, I was told to put this pea under the bottom one.
WIZARD. What? What? A pea underneath the twelve, which would make a bump that only a true princess

could feel. And feeling she would not sleep, and not sleeping would prove herself a princess!

PRINCE *(looks around at all of them).* Who would do such a thing to the one I truly love! *(NETTLE points at IVY who points at BRIAR who points at the QUEEN. QUEEN looks sheepishly at PRINCE.)* Mother?

QUEEN. I did listen to them. I couldn't stand it if you married the wrong woman. But what the Wizard says is true. If she couldn't sleep for a tiny dried pea under the mattress, and then couldn't even lie about it, she's the truest princess I've ever seen and I am ready to call her daughter! *(ROSE runs to QUEEN and embraces her, then runs to the PRINCE and holds his hand.)*

PRINCE. Then we shall be married this afternoon. *(The other three PRINCESSES start to sneak off.)*

PAGE. Uh, Your Majesties, what of these other three princesses?

QUEEN. Princesses? You call them princesses? Page, I call them serving girls. Take them off to milk the cows and bake the bread and do your bidding to prepare for the wedding feast!

WIZARD. You mean I can't turn them into toads?

QUEEN. Only if they misbehave. *(The three PRINCESSES groan and whine as the PAGE chases them offstage.)*

PRINCE. It's off to the chapel for us now.

PRINCESS ROSE. And time to live happily ever after.

WIZARD. The end! *(All bow.)*

END

SOMEWHERE, "Princess & the Pea"

Ric Averill

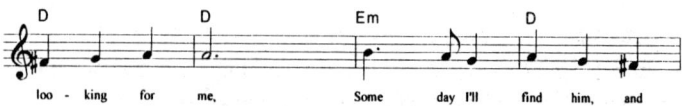

SOMEWHERE, Nightmare, "Princess & the Pea"

Ric Averill

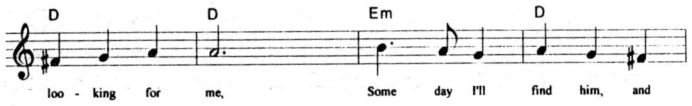

NO TV was first produced by the Seem-To-Be Players for a national tour in the spring of 1987. The production was directed by Ric Averill and included the following cast:

Serenity	SUSANNA PITZER
Mawm	DEDE DRESSER
Charley/ Theodore Bear/ Prince Charmin	JOHN NEWBOLD
The Dust Bee/ The Bed Bug/ The Underbedergator	JENNIFER GLENN

NO TV
a short play about imagination and cleaning

CHARACTERS

<u>The Real People</u>:
SERENITY: An imaginative 6-year-old girl.
CHARLIE: Her bratty little brother.
MAWM: Their mother.

<u>The Characters Who Arrive During the Cleaning of the Room</u>:
THE DUST BEE: A bee-like creature with a stinger.
THEODORE BEAR: A sweet enlargement of Serenity's teddy bear.
THE BED BUG: An annoying insect.
PRINCE CHARMIN: A handsome prince with toilet-paper epaulets.
THE UNDERBEDERGATOR: A wild monster-like creature.

<u>Doubling possible as follows</u>:
SERENITY
MAWM
CHARLIE / THEODORE BEAR / PRINCE CHARMIN
DUST BEE / BED BUG / UNDERBEDERGATOR

PLACE: Serenity's bedroom.
TIME: Just about any weekday after school.

SETTING: *Serenity's bedroom. She has a large TV which is sitting on top of a small chest, R. DR is a closet door with a large toy chest in front of it. LC is a bed. There is room for things and characters under it. Above the bed is a partial wall with a bulletin board filled with stuff. DL is the door through which MAWM enters and exits.*

AT RISE: *Lights come up on CHARLIE watching a violent action cartoon show on TV. The room is a mess. SERENITY enters.*

SERENITY. Hi, Charlie. *(No answer. He's absorbed.)* I said, Hi! Charlie. *(Another pause.)* You watchin' that again? When you gonna grow up? *(No answer.)* Charlie, I asked you a question!! Not supposed to be in my room watchin' TV, anyway. Why don't you watch the downstairs TV?

CHARLIE. Don't have to.

SERENITY. Anyway, I want to watch the *After School Special*. *(She changes the station.)*

CHARLIE. You can't do that! I was here first!!

SERENITY. But it's my room and my TV. Possession is nine-tenths of the law. *(She turns to sit down, CHARLIE hops up and changes channel.)*

CHARLIE. My show! And I wanna watch it!

SERENITY *(changes channel again)*. Go downstairs then!

CHARLIE. Can't! News is on! *(Changes it, a struggle begins.)*

SERENITY. It's my TV!

CHARLIE. It's both ours! It's just in your room!

SERENITY. Mine!

CHARLIE. Mine!

SERENITY. Creep!
CHARLIE. Brain-less!
SERENITY. Dummy!
CHARLIE. Dummy!

(As the fight picks up steam and they begin to push and shove, MAWM enters. She's been working all day and is tired.)

MAWM. What's going on in here?
CHARLIE. She hit me!
SERENITY. He hit me first!
CHARLIE. She's a half-brainer idiot!
SERENITY. Who's the idiot? You should see what *he* was watching on *my* TV.
CHARLIE. It's my TV, too, and I was watchin' it first. My show! My show! My show!!!
SERENITY. Baby!
CHARLIE *(breaks into tears)*. Am not!!
SERENITY. Cry-baby! *(He cries even more.)*
MAWM. That's enough!! Both of you, stop it right now! The TV's going off!!
SERENITY. No, it isn't.
CHARLIE. Not fair!
MAWM. You can't seem to agree on what to watch.
SERENITY. Yes, we can. My show!
CHARLIE. No, mine!
SERENITY. Mine!
MAWM. The TV is going off! *(She shuts it off.)*
CHARLIE & SERENITY. MAWWWWWWMMMMM!!!
MAWM. And it's going to stay off.
CHARLIE. It's your fault!

SERENITY. Uh-uh! Yours! Piggy!

MAWM. Serenity!

CHARLIE. Dummy!

MAWM. Knock off the name calling! Charlie, you go to your room right now!

SERENITY. Good riddance. Now I can watch my show. *(CHARLIE sticks out his tongue as he walks off.)*

MAWM. No, Serenity, I said the TV goes off and I meant it. For you, too.

SERENITY. Charlie's gone now. No one's going to argue over the channels.

MAWM. No TV, I said it and I mean it.

SERENITY. That's not fair!

MAWM. It's not fair that I have to come in here and settle your fights! Why don't you do something constructive for a change, or play with some of your hundreds of dollars worth of toys!

SERENITY. My toys are all old!

MAWM. So's the TV.

SERENITY. Please?

MAWM. No TV and that's final.

SERENITY. What am I gonna do?

MAWM. I've got an idea. Why don't you clean your room?

SERENITY. Mawm!

MAWM. That's a great idea. I'll bring you the vacuum cleaner!

SERENITY. I don't want to. I'll do it later!

MAWM. I didn't want to spend my evening disciplining you kids. I'll be right back!

SERENITY. My room's not messy! *(She kicks some toys around.)* It's not, it's not, it's not.

(MAWM reenters with a vacuum cleaner with a long extension cord. The Deluxe Filter Queen is a canister cleaner on wheels with multiple extensions sticking out from the top. It is an actual model, almost futuristic in design.)

MAWM. Ha! Tell it to someone who hasn't lived with you for six years! Now, you do a good job with this vacuuming, and then I'll let you have TV back. *(She exits.)*

SERENITY *(mimics her)*. "Then I'll let you have TV back"...hmmmph! What a bore! *(She sneaks up to TV and looks like she is going to turn sound down and TV back on.)*

MAWM *(from other room)*. And don't turn it on without the sound, either!

SERENITY. Guy, Mawm! I wouldn't do that! *(Goes over to toy bucket, lifts it up.)* Messy, messy, messy! *(Dumps out a toy, gets ready to dump entire thing.)*

MAWM. And don't make more mess, whatever you do!

SERENITY. Mawm! *(Mutters.)* Make messes if I want to!! *(Dumps bucket.)*

MAWM *(off)*. You mess it up, you vacuum it up!

SERENITY. "You mess it up, you vacuum it up!" I'll vacuum it up, all right. *(She turns the vacuum cleaner on. It whirs to life with a strange purring and immediately begins to take on a life of its own. She gets a determined look on her face and aggressively pushes her toys about with it. She stops, looks more closely at the cleaner. It is a silly machine and strikes her imagination. She begins to play. She takes off the end piece and puts her hand to it. The sound is stopped up and there is surprising suction against her hand. She laughs, then eyes her "rubber ducky" and holds the vacuum cleaner like a bazooka.)* Doom to the Rubber Ducky! *(She sucks up rubber ducky which sticks to the end of the cleaner. When she turns the vacuum off, the ducky drops into her toy box. She laughs and proceeds to "suck up" other toys and explode them into the bucket, "dooming" each.)* I'll clean it up all right. Clean up time, boys and girls! *(She continues "on and offing" toys.)* Dropping off the face of the earth! Boom! Crash!

(MAWM enters, stares at SERENITY.)

MAWM. Serenity, if you keep turning the vacuum cleaner on and off you'll burn out the motor! Either do it or don't do it!

SERENITY *(slightly embarrassed)*. I'm cleaning. Can I really have TV back if I do a good job?

MAWM. Yes, of course, but not if you ruin the vacuum cleaner, all right?

SERENITY. All right. Sorry.

MAWM. That's my girl.

SERENITY *(as MAWM leaves)*. The Doom Sucker Machine cleans up again. *(She turns on vacuum cleaner and crouches down behind it. She moves it slowly right like a tank, making battle noises. She approaches the TV and begins to poke behind it, sticking the bare nozzle offstage.)* All right, you're covered now. Come on out of there! *(Something yanks on the nozzle, she almost drops it, tugs back. There is a brief tug of war.)* What's going on back there?

(She gives a firm yank and THE DUST BEE comes buzzing out, angrily buzzing back and forth. The creature is dressed in a bee suit with dust hanging everywhere, sort of like a dust bunny, except it's a bee with a stinger and stripes. SERENITY names it.)

SERENITY. A Dust Bee!!!

DUST BEE. Zzzzzzz, right. A dust bee! You can't clean me, can't clean me. No one can 'cause I'm the Dust Bee! Hee-hee-hee! Doom to cleanliness. Doom to cleaners!

SERENITY. Get back, you filthy insect! *(The BEE jumps up and turns, attacking her with its stinger extended. SERENITY backs off.)*

DUST BEE. Filthy insect! Filthy? I love being filthy! *En Garde*, Human Child!!

SERENITY *(grabs the long, corner cleaning attachment and swings it like a sword).* En garde! Take that! And that! And... *(They battle, SERENITY's "sword" striking the stinger of BEE. They make a large circle around the vacuum cleaner. Suddenly the BEE gets the better of her. SERENITY's "sword" falls to the ground and slides out of sight.)*

DUST BEE. There you see, there you see! You fall disarmed by the Dust Bee!!! Now to finish this filthy fight! *(BEE charges, but SERENITY rolls over and pulls up suddenly on the cord of the vacuum cleaner and the BEE trips and does a graceful slow-motion spin, falls on the toy chest, lands on the "sword" attachment, pops like a balloon and flies off, hissing and deflating like a balloon out of sight behind the TV. SERENITY releases the cord and it zips back inside the vacuum cleaner. She jumps, startled, then laughs at herself and picks up the ducky and speaks to it.)*

SERENITY. The Dust Bee is dusted and busted! And the kingdom is once more safe from evil and little rubber duckies can fly hither, thither and yon!! *(She throws the ducky up and catches it, then throws it left to behind the bulletin board. The ducky comes flying back out as if thrown.)* What's this? *(She tosses it again. It comes out again!)* All right. What's going on?

(She walks boldly back and tosses it, then quickly puts her hand behind the bulletin board and grabs THEODORE BEAR, pulling him out. She recognizes him instantly. He is a rather sheepish, over-sized teddy bear. As they talk, the BED BUG—a very annoying insect, big, obnoxious, slime-green and irritating—comes slinking out and gets onto SERENITY's bed and takes a relaxed pose.)

SERENITY. Theodore Bear, what are you doing hiding back there?
THEODORE BEAR. Shhhh. Shhh, you're going to give me away.
SERENITY. What are you talking about?
THEODORE BEAR. I am hiding!
SERENITY. Hiding? What do you mean, hiding?
THEODORE BEAR. I'm hiding from the Bed Bug! *(He points to the BUG, but SERENITY is too busy watching him to see the irritating thing.)*
SERENITY. The Bed Bug? Sure, Theodore, sure you're hiding from the Bed Bug. What are you talking about?

Let's play. I just got rid of the Dust Bee, so nothing's going to hurt you now.

THEODORE BEAR. It's not so much hurt. It's just—you know, the Bed Bug, it's really irritating.

SERENITY. Theodore Bear. You're supposed to keep *me* from being afraid and here you are whining about some imaginary Bed Bug! You are just— *(During this speech, THEODORE begins pointing at the BUG, who is posing and stretching. The BUG yawns rather loudly.)*

BED BUG. Yawn!

THEODORE BEAR. Look.

SERENITY *(turns and finally sees the BUG)*. What in the world? What are you doing in my bed?

BED BUG. I'm the Bed Bug, lady. Where'd you expect to find me, in the refrigerator? What a ninny! *(Hops up and pokes her in an irritating manner, then gets right in her face.)* Hey, you're kinda cute, for an ugly human.

SERENITY *(backs away from the BUG, who moves her attentions to THEODORE)*. Just who do you think you are? And why—

BED BUG. I think I'm the Bed Bug, at least I was the last time I looked. *(Looks at herself, grabs a small brush attachment from the vacuum cleaner and uses it as a microphone, singing.)* Look at me! I'm as Bed Buggy a Bed Bug as you'll see!

SERENITY. That's really awful singing.

BED BUG. Does it bug you? *(Gets in her face, pulls at her hair.)* Hey, when was the last time you washed your hair? *(Turns her attention to THEODORE, poking him.)* Let alone your teddy bear.

THEODORE BEAR *(backing off, irritated)*. I'm Theodore now. I've grown out of Teddy!

BED BUG. Hey, let's watch TV! *(BUG runs to the TV, SERENITY blocks her.)*

SERENITY. No!

BED BUG. Ha! *(BUG searches through the toy box.)* Better yet, let's watch a videotape of commercials over and over again. Just for fun. *(Stops flinging toys, noticing THEODORE.)* Hi, Teddy! *(Starts punching THEODORE.)*

THEODORE BEAR. Please, it's Theodore and leave me alone!!

BED BUG. Nonsense, you make a great punching bag. I never had a brother before, you know. *(Continues punching THEODORE lightly. THEODORE is really irritated and helpless. SERENITY is getting upset.)* Take this and this and that and that!

THEODORE BEAR. Serenity, stop this Bed Bug!

SERENITY. Stop it, Bed Bug! Don't punch on Theodore!

BED BUG. Sure enough, I'll just punch on you! *(Turns her attention to SERENITY, punching her.)* Hey, nice. Your brother musta been softening you up!! How's about that? Pow, pow! *(THEODORE hides behind SERENITY's back. SERENITY backs away from the BUG and bumps into the vacuum cleaner. She looks down and gets an idea.)*

SERENITY. Wait a minute. OK, OK, you win. You like punching bags? Do you?

BED BUG. Sure, you know I do. They're great and you're the greatest! Pow! Pow!

SERENITY. Guess what?

BED BUG. What?

SERENITY. Guess what?

BED BUG. What?

SERENITY. I've got the best punching bag ever right here. *(She lifts the lid of the vacuum cleaner and pulls out the bag. The BUG looks at her with great curiosity.)*
BED BUG. You think I'm going to trust you?
THEODORE BEAR. She's very trustworthy.
SERENITY. This is a Deluxe Filter Queen bag.
BED BUG. Oh?
SERENITY. And it will be very, very irritated if you punch it!!
BED BUG. The Deluxe Filter Queen won't like it!?
SERENITY. Not at all.
BED BUG. Hey, this I gotta see! *(The BUG rears back and punches the bag hard. Of course, the bag exudes a great amount of dust which chokes up the BUG who runs off screaming!)* Pow! Yaaarrrrgh!! Dust bunnies! Eeeks! Sneeze, wheeze! I'm exterminated. Help!!

(MAWM enters, sees SERENITY holding the "smoking" bag.)

THEODORE BEAR. Good work, Serenity! *(He notices MAWM and freezes like a stuffed animal.)*
SERENITY. Victory once more for—
MAWM. Serenity! What have you done! *(SERENITY looks "caught," drops the bag to the floor.)* If you needed to change the bag, why didn't you call me? Look at this mess. And what are you doing playing with your teddy bear when you're supposed to be—
THEODORE BEAR *(mumbles)*. Theodore.
MAWM. —cleaning your—
SERENITY. Mawm. I was just checking the bag. I'll clean it up. I really will— *(Turns to get support from THEO-*

DORE, but he is busy exiting.) Theodore and I were just—never mind. Come on, Mawm, I'll get it clean.

MAWM. All right, you better. I don't want any more nonsense or extra messes. I'd think you'd just want to get it cleaned straight away. *(She exits. SERENITY replaces the bag in the vacuum cleaner, turns it on and goes to work. She works a bit, then gets distracted and begins to dance with the cleaner. She laughs.)*

SERENITY. Shall we dance, tra-la-la-la— *(She stops and is working on a particularly hard place. She stops, looks for something.)* Where is that attachment for corners? Where did it go? *(She looks about, works cleaner as though trying to vacuum up the extra missing attachment. She shoves the cleaner into dresser, under TV, and then under her bed. When she pulls it out, a dress is caught by the suction. She holds the dress up to herself, then shuts off the cleaner and sits on it.)* Oh, my old party dress. I'll wear it... *(She stands, spins around the dress, holding it to herself.)* I'll wear it, to the ball. Sorry, Charles, you're too young to go to the ball! Only beautiful princesses—but, of course, I'm not a princess, just a poor cleaning girl—who just for one magical night might...

(As she is trying on the dress and doing her Cinderella bit there is a fanfare of music and out from the behind the TV area steps PRINCE CHARMIN. He is dressed in a grand style and wears two rolls of toilet paper velcroed to his shoulders for epaulets.)

SERENITY. My, oh, my! What's this?

PRINCE CHARMIN. Good day, fair maiden. I am the noble Prince Charmin— *(Bows and winks.)* —squeezably soft, as it were. I have been traveling the countryside far and wide.

SERENITY. Oh, and whatever for?

PRINCE CHARMIN. My dear, last night, at the ball, a beautiful young maiden, such as yourself, arrived at the palace in a coach of gold. I danced and danced with her, but at midnight, yeah, verily, at midnight, the coach disappeared and in its place there was a small Deluxe Filter Queen vacuum cleaner looking very much as this one does. Soon it too disappeared, rolling down the road with the princess aboard it. But, as it bumped over the cobblestones, this...this attachment for corners fell off. *(He presents it formally.)*

SERENITY. Oh. *(Sheepishly recognizing her attachment.)*

PRINCE CHARMIN. So, I have been looking across the kingdom, yeah, verily, to find the princess with the Deluxe Filter Queen vacuum cleaner with the missing attachment for corners. Might I try yours?

SERENITY. Why, it is a Deluxe Filter Queen! And I am missing my attachment for corners!

PRINCE CHARMIN. For corners? Then it must be...it must be... *(He places the attachment on top of the vacuum cleaner and it fits.)* It is. It fits. You are my one true princess!!! *(He bows and kisses her hand.)* M'lady, let me roll out the carpet to my castle! *(He takes the toilet paper off his shoulders and "rolls" out the carpet. Two long strands of toilet paper roll across the floor. SERENITY is flattered.)*

SERENITY. Oh, my, I just don't know what to say. I'm just...

(PRINCE CHARMIN backs off stage as MAWM walks in, surprising SERENITY.)

SERENITY. I'm just... *(Notices MAWM.)* Uh, hi, Mawm.
MAWM. Serenity, what are you doing now? What could have possibly possessed you to roll out to their full lengths not one, but two rolls of toilet paper? This I might expect of Charlie, but you, you're older and—
SERENITY. It wasn't me, it was Prince— *(Turns to find him, but he's gone. She comes up with an excuse and collects the toilet paper rapidly.)* Uh, well, I was just going to dust with them. I couldn't find any dust cloths so, I thought I'd just—come on, Mawm! Just leave me for a few more minutes and I promise I'll get the room cleaned up, OK?
MAWM. All right, but no more shenanigans. *(She shakes her head and leaves. PRINCE CHARMIN puts his head back in.)*
PRINCE CHARMIN. I didn't know you had a mawm!
SERENITY. Some help you are.
MAWM *(from off)*. And don't forget to get under the bed!!
SERENITY. Under the bed?
VOICES *(from all over)*. Under the bed.
PRINCE CHARMIN. Under the bed? Gee, I gotta go!
SERENITY. What do you mean you gotta go?
PRINCE CHARMIN. I don't want to face the...the...the Underbedergator!! *(He exits quickly. SERENITY looks around, slowly absorbing what he has just said.)*
SERENITY. The Underbedergator?
VOICES. The Underbedergator. *(SERENITY approaches the bed, hooking up the vacuum cleaner. She turns it on and pushes the end of it under bed. The extension on it is pulled off as it goes under and she yanks it back.)*
SERENITY. What? *(She puts a new extension on the end of the vacuum cleaner. She moves it under bed and ex-*

tension #2 is pulled off. The same thing happens with a third extension and she is left with just a short brush.) What is going on? It couldn't be the...

(SERENITY lifts the edge of the bedspread and the UNDERBEDERGATOR grabs at her. She jumps back, but UNDERBEDERGATOR leaps out from under the bed, jumps on top of it and begins to throw the extensions at her. The UNDERBEDERGATOR is a big purple bully who looks a bit like a monster, but more ridiculous than scary. SERENITY dodges the extensions.)

UNDERBEDERGATOR. Yes, the Underbedergator! It's me! Usually ready to grab a loose hand or foot at night. But today, I stir angry as you poke and prod with your Deluxe Filter Queen. Yes, you, Serenity, shall have serenity no more!! Arrrgh!! *(UNDERBEDERGATOR stretches to its full height and roars.)*

SERENITY. You can't get me. I'll vacuum you to extinction. I will.

UNDERBEDERGATOR. Ha! Never. I know about electricity! *(Hops down and unplugs the vacuum cleaner!)* Aaaaarrrgh! *(UNDERBEDERGATOR chases her. Around they go, and she ducks so it races past her. SERENITY trips it up a bit.)*

SERENITY. Take that! I'll doom you like I did the Rubber Ducky because— *(She grabs its tail and swings it toward the TV.)* —I know about electricity, too! *(She plugs the vacuum back in and chases UNDERBEDERGATOR. As she does, she is thoroughly cleaning the room without knowing it. UNDERBEDERGATOR is on the run.)* Take that and that! I said I'd clean this room and I'm going to do it!! Victory!!!

(She is about to corner UNDERBEDERGATOR when MAWM enters the room. MAWM can't see UNDERBEDERGATOR, who proceeds to threaten MAWM behind her back. MAWM is oblivious to it all.)

MAWM. I'll say almost victory, dear. This is looking very nice.

UNDERBEDERGATOR. Arrgh, ruff, eat Mawm!!! Ha! *(It charges MAWM who moves away just in time and inspects the collection of toys and general cleanliness of the room.)*

SERENITY. Uh, Mawm, I think you better—

MAWM. It just shows what productive things can be done when you take away TV. *(Again, UNDERBEDERGATOR charges MAWM and misses. SERENITY is trying in a futile way to get MAWM's attention on UNDERBEDERGATOR, but MAWM is far more concerned with congratulating SERENITY on the cleanliness of the room.)*

SERENITY. Mawm, I was just about to, uh—you better—

UNDERBEDERGATOR. Get you, eat you, snurfle, Mawm, you eliminated— *(Another near miss.)*

MAWM. Oh, I see, honey, you haven't finished under the bed. Closet looks good, behind bulletin board—

SERENITY. Mawm—

UNDERBEDERGATOR *(last miss, as MAWM gets up from looking under the bed)*. Mawm sandwich!!

SERENITY. Mawm— *(Pushes MAWM out of harm's way.)*

MAWM. Oh, I get it, Serenity. You don't want me to come in until you're done. No problem. I'll be back in just a minute, then, dear. *(Exits just as UNDERBEDERGATOR tries one last lunge. SERENITY faces off UNDERBEDERGATOR, then:)*

SERENITY. Oh, no you don't, Underbedergator. You're finished! *(Charges, UNDERBEDERGATOR struggles, but is glopped by the sucking end of the vacuum cleaner. UNDERBEDERGATOR, like any bully defeated, begins to scream, cry and blubber.)*

UNDERBEDERGATOR. That hurts! Not fair, dummy! I don't like you. *(Grabs a bizarre suitcase from under the bed.)* I'm moving, I'm never speaking to you again. I'm running away and not coming back. So there! *(Runs off.)*

SERENITY. Mawm! Mawm! I did it! I'm free. I did it. The room's clean!

(MAWM enters, CHARLIE behind her.)

MAWM. Why, so it is, dear. So it is. I knew you could do it. Now you can watch TV just as much as you want to. Go ahead. Gee, maybe I'll even take a break and watch a show with you.

SERENITY. Watch TV? Mawm!? You gotta be kiddin'. I don't want to watch TV. I'm gonna go clean Charlie's room! *(MAWM and CHARLIE stare at her dumbfounded. SERENITY giggles and runs off, dragging the vacuum cleaner behind her. Blackout.)*

END

CATS AND BATS was first produced by the Seem-To-Be Players in Lawrence, Kan., October 1997. The production was directed by Ric Averill and included the following cast:

Lucy	JENNIFER GLENN
Nolan	ERIN KESSLER
Belfry	MATT CHAPMAN
Ranger	RIC AVERILL

CATS AND BATS

CHARACTERS

NOLAN: A little girl, 6.
LAZY LUCY: Her cat.
BELFRY: Her new bat.
RANGER: The mean dog down the street.

> PLACE: Nolan's backyard.
> TIME: Today, near Halloween.

SETTING: *Nolan's backyard includes a door, a fence, a comfy sleeping place for LUCY, and a tree for BELFRY to perch upon. This can either be realistic or suggested with platforms, boxes and levels. The original production was done "on the set" of a Halloween production for older children.*

AT RISE: *Lights come up as NOLAN comes out of her house and looks around the yard. She calls for her cat.*

NOLAN. Lucy! Lazy Lucy! Where are you?

(Lights come up on her relaxed cat, sleeping nearby. LAZY LUCY is calico and very complacent. She is as content and spoiled as she is warm and furry.)

LUCY. Am I hearing you, Nolan? No, I'm not hearing you. *(She goes back to sleep.)*

NOLAN. Lucy, I have something important to tell you!

LUCY. Do I hear food in that sentence? Does anyone hear a reference to food? I don't believe so. I'm still not hearing you.

NOLAN. Lucy, I'll get you some sardines if you come out! *(LUCY leaps up and scrambles down to NOLAN and curls herself against NOLAN's feet. NOLAN does not understand the animals, perceiving their conversation as mews, squeaks and barking.)*

LUCY. Hello, Mistress Nolan, I live to obey! *(Looks up and mews.)* Where's the sardines?

NOLAN. Ha, you're such a sucker.

LUCY. No sardines? *(Another mew. NOLAN laughs.)*

NOLAN. I'll have Dad get you some at the store. *(LUCY starts off.)* Don't go, Lazy Lucy. I have big news. You're going to have a new baby brother. *(LUCY looks back around, curious.)*

LUCY. Are you my mother? You are my mother, but you are not a mother cat. You cannot have kittens. I am not understanding you, Nolan. *(NOLAN kneels down and rubs behind LUCY'S ears. LUCY purrs.)*

NOLAN. My dad said I could have any pet from his lab, and so I chose a bat, which he says I can keep for a while, till it gets too big, but it eats fruit flies and stuff, and insects and we'll feed it so it stays around and build it a little house where it can live upside down and you and the bat, whose name is going to be Belfry, can be best friends. Like brother and sister.

LUCY. Brother. I can't believe you're telling me this. What if I say no?

NOLAN. I knew you'd be excited. I'm going right now to pick up Belfry! *(She exits, then sticks her head back out.)* Oh, yeah, here's a steak bone Mom says is big enough for you to chew on. *(She tosses LUCY a bone, then exits.)*

LUCY. Great. I get told I'm going to have to share everything with a newborn brother, and then you throw me a bone. What is a bat, anyway? I've had the neighbor boys chase me with a baseball bat, but it can't be that. They don't eat fruit flies. I am not understanding this. Ah, well, time to see if Nolan left me as small a portion of meat as usual.

(A big mean dog, RANGER, leaps on and stares at LUCY. He growls.)

RANGER. Hello, Lucy. I see it's dinner time.
LUCY. Darn it, Ranger, get out of here. Doesn't your master ever feed you anything?
RANGER. Of course, but not enough. And your steak bone smells so fine. I know you love to share, as you're such a good cat.
LUCY. Don't good cat me. Go get your own bone. I'm eating. *(RANGER suddenly leaps toward her, grabs the bone and runs off laughing.)*
RANGER. Thank you, so much. Thank you, thank you, thank you, Lucy. You are so generous, so gracious... *(He laughs as he exits.)*
LUCY. And so hungry. This is not a very good day. First I find out I'm going to have a baby brother and I don't even know what variety he's going to come in and now I've given away, whether I like it or not, my special

steak bone. I think I'll just curl up in the sun and sleep off my troubles.

(She moves to her original position and gets ready to sleep. Suddenly there is a flurry of activity as NOLAN enters with BELFRY, the bat, who has a tremendous amount of energy. BELFRY flies around the yard, LUCY looks up, surprised. NOLAN giggles.)

BELFRY. Wowie, kazowie, and bam-sh-bam, what a great backyard! I smell a fly, as good to the taste buds as a free French fry! I'm in love with this place. I am. I'm in love with you, Nolan. *(BELFRY swoops down to NOLAN and gives her a quick kiss, then flies around.)*

NOLAN. You silly bat. I can't believe how excited you are.

BELFRY. Excited doesn't begin to explain the joy I feel to be free of the lab. You and me gonna be great pals, Nolan! Hmmmm, I see a mosquito! *(BELFRY "flies" rapidly across the stage, grabs a bug and eats it, much to LUCY's disgust and NOLAN's amusement.)*

LUCY. I cannot believe what I am seeing. It is a hyperactive, bug-eating, flying mouse! This thing has got to go. *(She curls out of her place and moves quite quickly, taking a swipe at BELFRY.)* Hsssss.

BELFRY. Hu-woah! That's not so sweet! Back, lion.

NOLAN. Lucy, don't be so unfriendly. Belfry is your new brother and you have to share the backyard with him.

LUCY. Oh, I don't think so. *(She chases after the bat, but BELFRY flies very high up and screeches.)*

BELFRY. Keep that vicious killer away from me! What kind of a home is this. I'm calling the SRS, the SPCA!

NOLAN. Calm down this instant, Lucy. I'll get you some food.
LUCY *(calming down)*. Sardines?
NOLAN. Maybe I can even find those sardines I promised you. Come on, Belfry, I have some fruit flies inside for you and I want to show you your new inside mansion. *(BELFRY flies down to her hand and follows her in, sticks out his tongue at LUCY.)*
BELFRY. Later, kitty.
LUCY. New mansion. I hope your new mansion is a cage like my travel box. I can't believe it.

(NOLAN sticks her head back out and sets down a plate with a few leftover fish sticks on it.)

NOLAN. Here, Lucy, no sardines, but Charlie's leftover fish sticks didn't get thrown away yet. *(She darts her head back inside.)*
LUCY. I am the victim of my own good nature. The fact that I am here, day after day, being my lovely self, has assured me that Nolan no longer finds me amusing. She used to play with me, drag bits of string past my nose for me to chase ...

(RANGER enters and looks at her, then at the fish sticks.)

RANGER. And pull your tail so hard you could be heard screeching for miles. I see it's snack time.
LUCY. Ranger, go get your own leftover fish sticks.
RANGER. No toddlers in my house. The teenagers I live with eat everything, and then more. I'm so happy you

decided to share! Ha! *(He roars down and barks at her, steals the food, and then bounds off.)*

LUCY. This is singularly the worst day of my life. What else could possibly go wrong?

(NOLAN opens the door and shoos BELFRY out.)

NOLAN. Go out and play, Belfry, since you don't like it in the cage. Daddy promised a better outdoor home for you when he gets back. You can play with Lucy. *(LUCY looks at NOLAN, then at BELFRY.)*

LUCY. Now I *know* what else can go wrong.

BELFRY. Hey, baby!

LUCY. My name's Lucy, and according to our Mistress Nolan, *you* are the baby.

BELFRY. Don't think so. I got the wings, so I can do circles over your head. So I must be older, 'cause I'm higher.

LUCY. Yeah, well get down here and see who's bigger, you overgrown, winged bug eater.

BELFRY. Mustn't call names. *(He zooms down and she swipes at him.)* Missed me. *(He flies up higher again.)* How come you're so grumpy?

LUCY. Do I seem grumpy?

BELFRY. Uh, wait, thinking for a minute. Hmmmm, swiping at me, whining all the time...yes, you do.

LUCY. This is only the worst day of my life.

BELFRY. Maybe I can cheer you up. It's the best day of mine.

LUCY. Oh, why?

BELFRY. I got out of the laboratory, I moved in here, free fruit flies, and I got a fab new friend... *(Flies down to her, she swipes at him.)*
LUCY. I'm not your friend.
BELFRY. I know, but Nolan is. Which leaves you... hmmm, shall we say, friendless.
LUCY. Thank you for pointing it out.
BELFRY. I feel sorry for you.
LUCY. I don't want pity.

(BELFRY flies up high. NOLAN comes out with a large box, which she sets up high. LUCY tries to get her attention, rubbing against her leg.)

NOLAN. Here, Belfry, your night mansion. Lucy, don't be annoying.
LUCY. You used to like it when I rubbed against your leg.
BELFRY. She likes me now. I'm her hot Halloween item!
NOLAN. Poor kitty, are you jealous? *(Rubs behind her ears a moment.)* Oh, Daddy did bring your sardines. Let me get them. *(She steps inside.)*
LUCY. See, she does still love me.
BELFRY. But you can't fly.

(NOLAN steps out, places sardines on a plate near LUCY.)

NOLAN. Here you are. Enjoy. I have to go practice piano. You two enjoy yourselves till I get back.
LUCY. Belfry, why don't you just fly your hot Halloween self right out of my way—unless you like sardines—in which case try to get them from me.

BELFRY. Too fishy. *(From very high.)* What's that big, ugly creature doing bounding over here?
LUCY. Oh, no, not Ranger! I have to hide the sardines!! Look out, Belfry, he bites!
BELFRY. I'm out of here.

(BELFRY hides in his box, peeking out and witnessing the next scene. LUCY is pushing the sardines to the side of the stage. RANGER bounds on.)

RANGER. Ha! That's the best-smelling snack yet. Sardines.
LUCY. They're not yours! *(Mews loudly.)* Nolan! Get this mutt out of our backyard!
RANGER. Mutt! I'm about the purest bred dog you ever saw. Pure mean, pure nasty and pure hungry. You'd best get away from those sardines or I'll bite your tail off.
LUCY. It's just not fair. You didn't rub against her leg. You didn't lie in the sun puddle and look cute. What did you do to deserve these sardines?
RANGER. I was born big and born bad, so I get what I want when I want it. *(He growls. BELFRY peeks out, shakes his head, then flies down and pinches RANGER on the back and flies back out of sight.)* Yee-ouch. What was that?
LUCY *(realizing she has a conspirator)*. What? I didn't see anything.
RANGER. Gnats or something. Give me the sardines.
LUCY. No. *(She hisses and strikes out at him. He goes for the sardines, but BELFRY flies by and strikes again. RANGER spins around and snaps. BELFRY flies right past LUCY.)*

BELFRY. Think Halloween. *(BELFRY hides.)*
RANGER. What was that?
LUCY *(looking at BELFRY, then RANGER)*. Uh, ghosts. Turns out this yard is haunted by mouse-ghosts!
RANGER. Mouse-ghosts? Ha, just oversize mosquitoes. The sardines. *(BELFRY flies by again and pokes RANGER who spins around and snaps and snaps.)* What do you mean, mouse-ghosts?
LUCY. I once picked on a mouse, the same way you pick on me. And then, when he died, he turned into a flying mouse-ghost. I'm miserable half the time.
RANGER. I don't believe you.
LUCY. See. *(She does a dance like she's being picked on.)* Ouch. Ouch. Ouch. Ouch! *(RANGER starts to laugh. BELFRY swoops down and starts poking RANGER.)*
BELFRY. Ooooooooo, mean things get what mean things give!
RANGER *(dancing and leaping, trying to avoid the poking)*. Help, mouse-ghosts! Mouse-ghosts! Mouse-ghosts! What do you do to get them off?
LUCY. Nothing, sometimes it lasts for days. The only way to keep them off is to stay away! The mouse-ghost stays in this yard!
RANGER. Ouch, off me! Ouch! Off! All right, I'll leave, I'll leave! Help! Yelp! *(He barks and runs offstage. BELFRY follows a short distance then lets up his attack. LUCY looks up at BELFRY.)*
LUCY. I suppose you think I'm going to thank you.
BELFRY. It wouldn't surprise me.
LUCY. Well, thank you. Do you want a sardine?
BELFRY. No. *(Pause.)* You know what I do want?
LUCY. What?

BELFRY. I want it to be true. What you said.

LUCY. What did I say?

BELFRY. You said mouse-ghosts stay in this yard. I want you to let me stay here.

LUCY. Really?

BELFRY. I want you to be my friend.

LUCY. I'm not sharing my sardines.

BELFRY. That's OK. I don't like sardines, but I do like those gnats that swarm around them. *(He swoops down and picks off some gnats. LUCY eats. They both go yummmmmmm.)* Yummmmmmm.

LUCY. Yummmmmmm. *(She moves up to her place. Looks at BELFRY.)* I always get sleepy after I eat.

BELFRY *(flitting around)*. Me, too.

LUCY. Then come here, little brother. There's room in this sun puddle for both of us.

(BELFRY cuddles up to LUCY, a light shines brightly on both of them. NOLAN comes out of her house and looks up at them.)

NOLAN. Hmmm, who would have thought that cats and bats would get along so well. *(She blows them both a kiss.)* Good night and Happy Halloween.

END

THE GREAT ALPHABET ROBBERY was first produced by the Meade Hall Players in Lawrence, Kan., in February 1974. The production was directed by Jeanne Averill and included the following cast:

Principal/ Uncle Chimmie Toots	JEFF DEARINGER
Ms. Picadilly	JEANNE AVERILL
Oscar	DAVID NASTER
Archibald	ROGER NOLAN
Letters	TERE LEE, BETH JOHNSON, DIANE CUTLER, DALE WILSON, TINA WILSON

THE GREAT ALPHABET ROBBERY
a play in seven short scenes

CHARACTERS

PRINCIPAL/UNCLE CHIMMIE TOOTS: A magical mysterious man.
MS. PICADILLY: A frustrated teacher.
OSCAR: A precocious first-grader.
ARCHIBALD: His ne'er-do-well friend.
OTHER STUDENTS (4-14 in number)
ALPHABET LETTERS
    T
    D
    B
OTHER LETTERS (4-14 in number)

PLACE: An elementary school,
the Blue Hallway and Alphabet Land.
TIME: The present.

SETTING: *A school classroom C, featuring a chalkboard, a teacher's desk and 6-16 chairs. Cutouts of the alphabet are strung along the back wall. UR on a platform is the Principal's office represented by a desk and two chairs. DL is an odd door with a blue glow behind it, representing the Blue Hallway which leads to Alphabet Land. Alphabet Land, can be shown by draping the desks and chairs with fabric and blankets to form an "enchanted forest." Settings should be minimal and flexible.*

SCENE ONE — The Classroom

(There is a bell and the empty, first-grade classroom quickly fills with students shouting and laughing and pushing each other. The last two students to enter are ARCHIBALD, tall and smooth, and OSCAR, short and befuddled. Clearly friends, they saunter in, moving in tandem, look about and, from their back pockets, pull out plastic jars of bubbles and begin to blow. The OTHER STUDENTS jump in the air trying to pop the bubbles. The teacher, MS. PICADILLY, a rather nervous young woman who would probably be better off in retail, enters, takes one look at the chaos and turns, leaving the center area to approach the principal's office, UL.)

SCENE TWO — The Principal's Office

(PRINCIPAL is seated on a swivel chair with his back to the audience, playing a small tin whistle. When MS. PICADILLY knocks on the door, he quickly sets down the whistle, but does not turn, seeming instead to simply "know" who is there. He speaks with a grave, matter-of-fact voice.)

PRINCIPAL. Come in, Ms. Picadilly.
MS. PICADILLY. Yes, sir. I'm in, sir.
PRINCIPAL. And how are things in the classroom?

MS. PICADILLY. Uh, fine...actually, not so fine. That's what I came to see you about.
PRINCIPAL. The problem?
MS. PICADILLY. It's Oscar and Archibald, sir. I can't seem to teach them a thing.
PRINCIPAL. Oh?
MS. PICADILLY. Yes, and it's especially difficult to teach them the alphabet. I've tried and I've tried. *(Gets more and more agitated.)* I've tried dittos, games, blocks, chalkboards, notebooks, yelling, screaming, threats... *(Recovering.)* Excuse me. As you can see, they're giving me a nervous condition. What can I do?
PRINCIPAL. Only one thing to do. If they misbehave again, send them to me.
MS. PICADILLY. Yes, sir.
PRINCIPAL *(in a strange and slightly maniacal voice)*. Send them to me down the Blue Hallway.
MS. PICADILLY. The Blue Hallway? *(No answer.)* Yes, sir. Good day, sir.
PRINCIPAL. Good day.

(She exits. PRINCIPAL swivels to face the audience, revealing that he is actually UNCLE CHIMMIE TOOTS. Underneath his suit coat is a pair of engineer overalls. His tie has antique railroad train engines on it and as he straightens the tie, he reaches down and puts on a conductor's hat, then exits.)

SCENE THREE — The Classroom

(OSCAR, ARCHIBALD, and the other STUDENTS are talking and horsing around. MS. PICADILLY enters, observes and becomes agitated.)

MS. PICADILLY. Quiet... Please, be quiet... class! *(Shouts and then removes her shoe and bangs it on the desk.)* QUIET!! *(They settle down. She is momentarily embarrassed by her outburst, then recovers.)* That's better. Today, class, we will study the alphabet... the first letter is A. Everybody say A.

STUDENTS. A.

MS. PICADILLY. Now, everybody say B.

STUDENTS *(all but OSCAR and ARCHIBALD, who are busy whispering)*. B.

MS. PICADILLY. Now we say C. *(Notices the whispering.)*

STUDENTS. C.

MS. PICADILLY *(moving in on the culprits)*. Oscar, what were you saying to Archibald? Would you like to share your thoughts with the entire class and see if they find them as interesting as the alphabet.

OSCAR. Surely. I just told the noble Archibald that I have a computer program at home to teach *me* the alphabet.

ARCHIBALD. Oscar was worried that *you* might be put out of a job.

OSCAR. Yeah. Kids learn faster from computers, and computers don't yell.

ARCHIBALD. Mine does.

MS. PICADILLY. Well, well, well, is that so? Tell me, Oscar, can you say the alphabet?

OSCAR. Sure.

MS. PICADILLY. Say it then.

OSCAR. It then.

MS. PICADILLY. No, the alphabet. Say the alphabet.

OSCAR. The alphabet.

MS. PICADILLY. Oscar, you will stay after school every day until you learn to be less insolent. *(ARCHIBALD raises his hand.)* Yes, Archibald.

ARCHIBALD. What does insolent mean?

MS. PICADILLY. Insolent is when you talk back or refuse to cooperate.

ARCHIBALD. Oh, that's terrible. *(With a certain sarcasm.)* Oscar, you should be ashamed of yourself. *(OSCAR hangs his head in shame.)*

MS. PICADILLY. Archibald. Can you say the alphabet?

ARCHIBALD *(starts to say "the alphabet" then thinks better of it)*. The...yes, I can.

MS. PICADILLY. Well?

ARCHIBALD. A B C D E F H I J...

MS. PICADILLY. Archibald, what happened to G?

ARCHIBALD. Gee, I dunno. *(Winks at OSCAR.)*

MS. PICADILLY. You may continue.

ARCHIBALD. You threw me off. A B C D E F G H I J K L M N O Q R S T...

MS. PICADILLY. Archibald, what happened to P?...Never mind. *(The BOYS look at each other and laugh, CLASS giggles.)* Archibald, you may continue. Start with P.

ARCHIBALD *(looks at OSCAR as though to say something, thinks better of it, goes on)*. P Q R S T U V W X...uh...

MS. PICADILLY *(frustrated, agitated)*. Y.

OSCAR. Yeah, why?

ARCHIBALD. Why not?
MS. PICADILLY. Y Z!
ARCHIBALD. Why not Z?
MS. PICADILLY. No! Y, Z, don't you see?
OSCAR, ARCHIBALD, STUDENTS *(getting into the rhythm of it, the class gets out of control).* Y, Z, don't you see! Y, Z, don't you see! Y, Z, don't you see! *(They continue until MS. PICADILLY shouts them.)*
MS. PICADILLY. Quiet...class...please, be quiet... Quiet!! *(Shouts and pounds her desk, collapses in tears, then looks up and smiles. An eerie silence fills the room.)* Oscar. Archibald. Both of you are to go to the office, right now.
ARCHIBALD. Y?
OSCAR. It's not why, it's the principal of the thing.
MS. PICADILLY *(stands and looks down at them, murder in her heart).* Now. Oh, and go by way of the Blue Hallway. *(They both look at her, very curious and slightly nervous.)*
ARCHIBALD *(to OSCAR, exiting).* I think she means us.
OSCAR. Blue hallway? *(He follows ARCHIBALD, shaking his head.)*

SCENE FOUR — The Blue Hallway

(The lights turn slightly blue. OSCAR and ARCHIBALD cross under the arch into the "hall" DL, and seem a bit glum.)

OSCAR. Gee, I wish I was a genius like Thomas Edison.
ARCHIBALD. Yeah, or Beethoven.

OSCAR. You know, Edison was so smart they kicked him out of school.
ARCHIBALD. Yeah, kicked Beethoven out, too.
OSCAR *(getting defensive)*. Well, Edison invented the light bulb.
ARCHIBALD. So did Beethoven!
OSCAR. No way. Beethoven, uh, Beethoven wrote nine symphonies!
ARCHIBALD *(for the sake of arguing)*. So did Edison!

(They scuffle and suddenly bump heads, then smile and drop to the ground, leaning on each another. A sleepy mood is evoked as lights turn a deeper blue. After a moment, an eighteenth-century wig descends from above as does a partially bald wig. The BOYS slowly rise as if in a dream. OSCAR puts on the bald wig and ARCHIBALD puts on the formal wig.)

ARCHIBALD *(looking at OSCAR)*. Hey, what's happening? Why are we...?
OSCAR *(nods with a dawning realization that he is becoming "possessed")*. I am not Oscar. I am Thomas Edison!
ARCHIBALD. I was never Archibald. I am and always have been Ludwig van Beethoven!
OSCAR. Beethoven, pleased to meet you. I'm Edison.
ARCHIBALD *(playing the eccentric composer)*. What? Oh, yes, Edison, I've heard so much about you. Any good ideas lately? *(They drop into an eccentric patter.)*
OSCAR. Yes, Ludwig van, I've been thinking about the sad lot of children.
ARCHIBALD. Just which sad lot were you referring to, Thomas?

OSCAR. You know, school.

ARCHIBALD. Oh, yes, I see. Terrible. *(To the tune of Beethoven's 5th.)* "I can't stand school." *(Laughs.)* Hmmm, catchy.

OSCAR. It seems to me that the alphabet has something to do with it.

ARCHIBALD *(preaching)*. The alphabet is the root of all evil!

OSCAR *(at a revival meeting)*. Without the alphabet, no schools.

ARCHIBALD. Without schools, no rules.

OSCAR. Beethoven, I'm getting an idea. *(Seriously breaking through.)* What we must do is steal the letters of the alphabet!

ARCHIBALD. No schools, no rules... yes! But, my dear Edison, we can't run blindly into alphabet theft alone.

OSCAR. You're right, Beethoven. We don't even know where the alphabet is kept. We'll have to find a dupe to take us to Alphabet Land.

ARCHIBALD. A dupe... Edison, where will we find a dupe? *(A flyer flutters to the ground. OSCAR picks it up.)*

OSCAR. What's this?

ARCHIBALD *(grabs it from him, reads)*. "Now playing at the Bistro. Uncle Chimmie Toots!" *(They look at each other.)*

BOTH. Uncle Chimmie Toots?

ARCHIBALD *(continues to read)*. "Chief Engineer of the tin whistle, songs in every key from A to Z."

OSCAR. A to Z. Did you say songs from A to Z?

ARCHIBALD. I may have. This flyer certainly does.

OSCAR. Do you realize that A to Z encompasses the entire alphabet.

ARCHIBALD. If he knows A to Z, he may know where the letters live.

OSCAR. Very likely, van Beethoven. Let's attend the concert at the Bistro and approach this strange chap, shall we? *(Indicates exit.)*

ARCHIBALD. Let's. *(They leave.)*

SCENE FIVE — Backstage at the Bistro

(The scene transforms. Added to the blue lights are lights of all colors. The classroom desks are covered by multicolored fabric or a camouflage drop. UNCLE CHIMMIE TOOTS walks on stage carrying a bright ladder and a large net. He sets the net down at the foot of the ladder and climbs up to the top, plays his tin whistle, then sings.)

UNCLE CHIMMIE TOOTS.
"Eeee Iiii oh mm
Eeee Iiii oh mm
Did you ee-ver, i-ver, o-ver
In your leefe, life, loaf,
See the fee-mer fi-mer, for-mer
Take a weefe, wife, wofe!
Eeee, Iiii Oh mm
Eeee Iiii oh mm oh!"

(He stops singing and bows. There are cheers from "offstage" as OSCAR and ARCHIBALD enter and plant themselves at the foot of the ladder.)

UNCLE CHIMMIE TOOTS. Oh, I love that song, I love that song. *(As he descends the ladder, OSCAR reaches up and takes CHIMMIE TOOTS' hat off and puts it on his own balding head.)* Now, where's my hat. Old Uncle Chimmie Toots lost his hat again. *(OSCAR hands him back his hat. CHIMMIE TOOTS is amused and befuddled by the antics of the BOYS.)*

OSCAR. Rescued it for you, sir. Good day.

ARCHIBALD *(he and OSCAR looming over CHIMMIE TOOTS)*. How are you?

OSCAR. Aren't you the famous Uncle Chimmie Toots? Songs from A to Z?

ARCHIBALD. Fanciful, fantastic, entertainer of entire entourages of enfants?

OSCAR. We've read all about you. *(They give him no time to answer.)*

ARCHIBALD. My name is Beethoven, Ludwig van.

OSCAR. And I'm Edison, Thomas Edison, of light-bulb fame? Perhaps you've heard of us? *(CHIMMIE TOOTS attempts to interject.)*

ARCHIBALD *(interrupting)*. And even if not, we've heard of you.

OSCAR. We have a need...

ARCHIBALD. For you to lead...

OSCAR. A mission that will do more for children than you've ever done with all your entertaining. *(Again UNCLE CHIMMIE TOOTS tries to speak.)*

ARCHIBALD. What do you say?

OSCAR. He's not talkative.
ARCHIBALD. Just nod your head. *(CHIMMIE TOOTS shakes his head in bewilderment.)*
OSCAR. He agrees! *(CHIMMIE TOOTS shakes his head no.)*
ARCHIBALD. Congratulations, you are a brave soul.
UNCLE CHIMMIE TOOTS. What do I... did I...
OSCAR. We'll tell you what to do.
ARCHIBALD. Just lead us to Alphabet Land.
UNCLE CHIMMIE TOOTS *(confused)*. I was on my way there, once, but I got off track.
OSCAR. We're here to get you back on.
ARCHIBALD. Do as we say and you'll save the day.
UNCLE CHIMMIE TOOTS. But... but... but... but... *(He is protesting as they push him toward the Blue Hallway. Then suddenly he stops, looks them right in the eye and winks, in control again.)* OK. *(They all exit.)*

SCENE SIX — Alphabet Land

(T, D and B enter and dance about the stage. OTHER LETTERS may be seen in the corners and on the periphery. The letters each speak only in words which start with their letters.)

T. Two times two till twilight takes time.
B. Bad balls bounce by bad bulging birds.
D. Did David Dolittle displace dirty dimes?
T *(preparing to play elsewhere)*. Till tea-time. Ta-ta.
D *(not wanting T to go)*. Do delay.
T *(leaving, but reassuring)*. Tea-time!

B *(comforting D, but getting ready to leave)*. Be brave, boy.

D. Do dally.

B *(exiting)*. Bye-bye.

D *(sitting, lonely)*. Drat! D didn't desire droopiness.

(OSCAR, ARCHIBALD and CHIMMIE TOOTS enter, sneakily.)

OSCAR. There's D now. Go get him, Uncle Chimmie Toots!

UNCLE CHIMMIE TOOTS. You sure you boys want to do this?

ARCHIBALD. Certainly. This is your chance. Remember, the genius of Beethoven and Edison is behind you. *(They get behind him. Push him forward with his net. He turns.)*

UNCLE CHIMMIE TOOTS. Now, you wouldn't fool old Uncle Chimmie Toots, would you? I don't like to be made a fool of. This will help the dear little children, won't it?

OSCAR. Cross my heart.

ARCHIBALD. Hope to die.

OSCAR. We're so famous...

ARCHIBALD. Why would we lie?

UNCLE CHIMMIE TOOTS. Do you have any idea what will happen if we steal the letters?

OSCAR. What will happen is no school.

ARCHIBALD *(hushing OSCAR)*. Sh. No school today, which is why we can play with you, Uncle Chimmie Toots. Think of it as an adventure...

OSCAR. Yes, you're a cowboy...

ARCHIBALD. Stalking the wild letter...

UNCLE CHIMMIE TOOTS. Ooooooo, yes. I get it. Stalking the wild letter. *(He sneaks up and throws net over D.)*

D. Don't dare disturb D. Danger! Danger! Drats. Dummies. Delay. Don't dirty dog D. *(CHIMMIE TOOTS shoves D under the ladder and covers him with a blanket. D stops talking.)*

UNCLE CHIMMIE TOOTS. There. That's enough from you, _. *(Mouths "D.")* Hmmm, this is curious. I can't say _. *(Same experience. As ARCHIBALD, OSCAR and CHIMMIE TOOTS try to talk, they cannot use the letters they have stolen. This accumulates into very confusing speech patterns.)*

ARCHIBALD. In_ee_, it is curious. _on't you think so, E_ison. E_ison?

OSCAR. E_ison. Oooops. What's this? We can't say _, *(Also mouthing D.)* or _og, or _irt, or Satur_ay!

(Enter B.)

ARCHIBALD *(he and OSCAR notice new letter)*. Quick, Uncle C...

OSCAR. Grab that B!

UNCLE CHIMMIE TOOTS. Oh, boy, it's a B.

B *(not noticing them)*. Bubbly bottles, bubble bottles, bubbly... *(Continues babbling.)*

UNCLE CHIMMIE TOOTS *(sneaks and sings)*.
"Your Uncle Chimmie Toots loves to catch,
Any letter that he can snatch.
He loves to snatch them tall and small,
But B's he likes the best of all!" *(Nets B.)*

The Great Alphabet Robbery

B. Bad Boy! Beast, be better, but... *(CHIMMIE TOOTS stuffs B under blanket. B is quiet.)*

UNCLE CHIMMIE TOOTS. There. Are you satisfie_, _eethoven?

ARCHIBALD. Not _eethoven, _eethoven. Oh, no. I can't say _. *(Mouths B.)*

OSCAR. Too _a_, _eethoven. This is strange.

(T enters.)

T. Two times two times two... *(Continues twittering.)*

OSCAR. Look, here's another letter.

UNCLE CHIMMIE TOOTS. My favorite. My secon_ name starts with a T. Leave it to me. *(He slowly approaches T, who looks at him.)* Ttttttt, Here, ttttttt. *(He grabs T in net.)*

T. Take time to think! Terrible turkey! Tragedy! Tragedy!

UNCLE CHIMMIE TOOTS *(puts T away. Feeling triumphant)*. Look a_ me. I migh_ ge_ all the le__ers of _he alpha_e_ ... Hey, I can har_ly _alk.

ARCHIBALD. E_ison, our plan is going _a_ly.

OSCAR. _ee_hoven, we can har_ly _alk, ei_her.

ARCHIBALD & OSCAR *(in desperation)*. Uncle Chimmie _oo_s!

UNCLE CHIMMIE TOOTS. Uncle Chimmie _oo_s!? Uh, oh. *(Sings.)*
 "Your Uncle Chimmie _oo_s likes _o _alk
 An_ _ake a walk aroun_ _he _lock..."

I _hink you _oys are _oing some_hing no_ qui_e righ_.

OSCAR. We _i_n'_ know.

ARCHIBALD. I'm no_ really _ee_hoven.

OSCAR. An_ I'm no_ really E_ison.

UNCLE CHIMMIE TOOTS. I'm really Uncle Chimmie _oo_s, I _hink.

OSCAR. Face i_. We _lew i_.

ARCHIBALD. Now we're _oome_ _o soun_ like we can'_ _alk.

UNCLE CHIMMIE TOOTS. You _oys ough_ _o know _e_er. _e_er?

OSCAR. Help, Uncle C.

ARCHIBALD. Wha_ are we gonna _o?

UNCLE CHIMMIE TOOTS. Don'_ you fear, _oys. Uncle Chimmie _oo_s is here! *(Thinks, gets idea, then lets B out.)* You boys ough_ _o know be_er. *(Thinks, then lets T out.)* You boys ought to know better. *(Lets D out.)* Dandy. *(The LETTERS sulk and growl with their sounds in OSCAR and ARCHIBALD's direction. CHIMMIE TOOTS sings.)*

"Your Uncle Chimmie Toots likes to talk,
And take a walk around the block,
To visit the mice and shake their hands,
And survey all the wondrous lands!"

(He exits singing. LETTERS growl and menacingly move to surround ARCHIBALD and OSCAR.)

D. Dummies, dummies... *(Etc.)*

B. Bad boys, bad boys... *(Etc.)*

T. Terrible twosome, terrible twosome... *(Etc.)*

ARCHIBALD. But we didn't know what the letters were for.

OSCAR. We didn't do it. Chimmie Toots did! *(LETTERS close in and engulf the BOYS. Blackout.)*

SCENE SEVEN — The Blue Hallway

(Lighter blue lights come up on OSCAR and ARCHIBALD. They are leaning back to back as they were in first Blue Hallway scene. The classroom returns to normal. The BOYS slowly stir and wake as from a dream. In their hands are the letters T, D and B, which are no longer hanging among the group of letters stretched across the classroom. They look up to where the letters should be and move rapidly to tape them back into place. Enter PRINCIPAL, very seriously, his back to the audience. He is, of course, UNCLE CHIMMIE TOOTS, but respectably dressed.)

PRINCIPAL. Can I help you boys with something?
OSCAR. Uh, no sir, not at all, sir...
ARCHIBALD. We were just rearranging letters.
OSCAR. Making sure everything is in its place.
ARCHIBALD. Then we're going back to class...
BOTH. To study the alphabet! *(As they run off, PRINCIPAL turns and reveals that he has overalls on under his suit jacket. He pulls out his tin whistle and dances off, playing a merry melody.)*

END

EEE-III-OOO Song

Traditional

UNCLE CHIMMIE TOOTS SONG #1

Averill

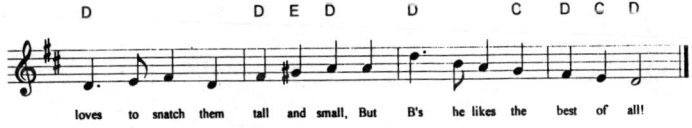

UNCLE CHIMMIE TOOTS SONG #2

Averill

UNCLE CHIMMIE TOOTS SONG #3

Averill

DIRECTOR'S NOTES